Dedicated to:

Aislinn
(Miss Tubby)

Special thanks to my Graphic Designer, Christina Lackowicz.
I couldn't have done this without you!

There was once a sloth cub named
Miss Tubby.

One day she was bored of hanging out in the trees. She really wanted some candy. She asks Mama Sloth for some candy.

Mama Sloth thought it was time that Miss Tubby learned about money to buy her own candy.

"What is money?"
asked Miss Tubby.

Mama Sloth, was deep in thought for two whole days.

Mama Sloth finally says to her sloth cub, "Miss Tubby, my dear, once upon a time not too long ago, there was a Sloth King."

"He was a wealthy sloth.
I remember his story and his wisdom.

He said, "some sloths think that being
rich is the answer to their problems.
There is a BIG difference between
being rich, and being wealthy."

He said, "The rich work very hard for their money, but the wealthy, have the power of choice and the freedom of time."

Sloth King continued, "The wealthy sloths do not have to climb down the trees daily to go to work. They can sleep, eat, and only come down from the trees when they want to."

"The sloths think of money as a destination, somewhere they can arrive at…"

"Do you want to know a secret?" asked the Sloth King, peacefully sitting on his throne surrounded by his favourite hibiscus flowers".

Miss Tubby slowly raises her hand, smiles, "YES!"

"Money is actually a tool. A tool for you to use. And what are tools used for?" Mama sloth paused, waiting for her sloth cub to answer.

"Tools are used to build things," answered Miss Tubby.

"Very good! Well done my love,"
Said Mama Sloth with so much joy,
she cried for two more days...

Mama Sloth continued, "The Sloth King agrees with you too, money is a tool used to build assets."

Miss Tubby looked confused, "But what are assets, mama?"

"Good question, Miss Tubby." Mama Sloth was proud of her sloth cub for asking the right questions.

"Well, you know how the Sloth King LOVES his hibiscus flowers? Think of assets as the endless supply of hibiscus flowers the Sloth King has."

"The Sloth King used money to build his own hibiscus garden. This took many years before he had a full field of hibiscus flowers, but once he did, he never had to buy another flower ever again."

"So...what are assets? Assets are what you build to never have to worry about money again. The Sloth King built a hibiscus garden so he didn't have to buy hibiscus from someone else using money." Mama Sloth continued.

"You see, Miss Tubby. Money is a tool we use to build wealth. We give it to others, we earn it through work, and trade it with others for things we want. Because we use money, the giving of money back and forth is called currency."

Mama Sloth looks at her sloth cub, "So, Miss Tubby, what do you think money is?"

Miss Tubby considers and slowly begins to answer mama sloth, "Money is what I can use to buy lots of hibiscus candy. I can sell half of the candy to my sloth friends, take the money I earned and buy one special hibiscus candy to grow so I can do it all over again. Right mama?!"

"Hahaha," mama sloth laughed, and laughed for two whole days.

Finally she said as she hugged her sloth cub, "Yes, Miss Tubby, that's what money is for."

About the Author

Queenie Wei is a social entrepreneur, investor, and wealth coach. She runs multiple businesses with her husband. This creation came from her desire to teach her own daughter about wealth from a young age. She believes that financial literacy *is* giving freedom back to the people, and hopes that many families will be able to connect with this story too to learn the difference between rich vs. wealthy.

- For more information check out our Facebook Group **Financial Literacy for the 99%** to level up your own financial literacy game and lay the foundation to generational wealth.

- Or visit: **Bonus.soulvibecapital.com/svc-5-cores-ebook-offer** to start your own wealth creation journey.

www.ingramcontent.com/pod-product-compliance
Lightning Source LLC
Chambersburg PA
CBHW042115040426
42448CB00003B/280